# Travellers
## An Introduction

*Jon Cannon*
*& the Travellers of Thistlebrook*

**Emergency Exit Arts/InterChange Books**

First published in 1989 by
InterChange Books and Emergency Exit Arts.
InterChange Books, 15 Wilkin Street, London NW5 3NG.
Tel: 01-267 9421.
Emergency Exit Arts, PO Box 570, Deptford, London SE8 3HL.
Tel: 01-853 4809.

CANNON, JON
  Travellers: An Introduction
  I. England. Social minorities. Itinerants. Social conditions.
  I. Title
  305. 5'68

ISBN 0-948309-14-8

Copies available from InterChange Books. Please send
payment with order, plus 70p (p&p).
Trade distribution by Turnaround Distribution, 27 Horsell
Road, London N5 1XL. 01-609 7836.
Cover photograph: Cherry Picking, Kent, 1989.
                    Liz Hildon and Cindy Harris.
Typeset by: Artworkers Typesetters, 402a St John Street,
London EC1V 4NJ.
Printed by: Lithosphere Printing Co-op, 203 Pentonville Road,
London N1.

# Contents

Foreword by Golia Anderson   7

Introduction by Debbie Mullins   11

**Part I**
*by Jon Cannon*

    i)      People who travel   19

    ii)     A History of Travellers in England   23

    iii)    Travellers Culture   33

**Part 2**
*by the Travellers of Thistlebrook*   43

    Further Reading   65

    Resources   67

    Acknowledgements   69

    References   71

I'll tell you what should be in the book. Don't let them open the book and read about hedgehogs, because that's all you ever see, they know that. Don't write about hedgehogs, write about the real things, y'know, ordinary things, that would make a good book.

It's like the difference between the movies in the afternoon and in the evening. Afternoons for kids, with all the pirates in silver and clean shaven. In the evening its the adults version and you get a bit more dirt, and different language.

You want to get some of the people who've seen a bit, tell 'em what you're doing. Don't tell them it's just about Gypsies or they'll tell you silly stuff. Explain it's serious, it's about them ordinary things. Then they'll tell you something real.

**John Harris**
**Thistlebrook**

# *Foreword*

**Two weeks spent on Thistlebrook site for Gypsies with
Emergency Exit Arts.**

Emergency Exit Arts are what we (Gypsies) call stu-
dent type people. They are a group of men and women who do all
types of different activities, and the fortnight they spent on
Thistlebrook with us was really enjoyable.

The children were the first to meet any of the
Emergency Exit Arts group, at least I think they were because I
can remember seeing the children with Debbie (one of the group)
before I even knew who she was, and I can also remember my little
boy Stevie telling me that the children from our site were going to
do a show; he said that we would all get a chance to see it because
they would be doing it on the site, which turned out to be true and
a good show it was too. So it was obvious that when the group first
came to stay on the site the children were the first to mix with
them, although the odd one or two grown ups did pop in to see
what was going on. I think the group thought that it might not turn
out the way it was supposed to at first, but after 3 or 4 days nearly
everyone had met them and the friendship grew from there. I say
friendship because that's the sort of way it seemed, they were all
real nice people.

There was quite a few students in the group but only
about six of them stayed here for the whole two weeks. They had a
large tent for living in and some portacabins for sleeping in. The

site has got some waste ground which we call the yards, the council cleaned part of these yards out, they are usually filled with rubbish which I must add is not all to be blamed on the residents, anyway this is where the group lived for the whole fortnight. They got their water and electricity from Aunt Bubbles (a resident) as she was nearest to them, and she got on quite well with the group as we all did.

The two weeks they spent on the site was during the school summer holidays, which gave the children something to do everyday. This was really good for the kids because the site has no facilities for the children at all and when you think that the site is meant to be one of the largest in England, and the children are definitely the majority on here then you must be able to understand the need for a play area. The group gave the children something different to do every day, and the children loved it in the yards with these people as did the grown ups, well they seemed to anyhow. The group would light a fire of an evening and the grown ups would sit talking for hours.

One of the first things the group did was to get some of the children together and with the group they danced to music all round the site. The children were dressed up in different colour clothes and they also had make up on. One of the men who was in the group was dressed up in a chicken's outfit. His name was Jonky. He played the part of the chicken very well and it was to be in a few more shows before they left the site. The children had made some flags and they were waving them around. The show was really colourful as it paraded around the site. The video camera ended up being on nearly every day, and there was quite a few laughs on the film when it was shown.

The group started a sort of play which the children were to act in. It was about a circus and some of the children were acting as different kinds of animals. The children were taught by different members of the group what they had to do. On the night the play was to be shown the children told their parents and relatives and everyone went in the yard. By the time the circus started the yard was packed with parents and families of the children. It was really good and people clapped and cheered for the children and the group, who had done a real good job. After the play was shown the group set a lot of tables up inside the tent, and everyone had a party. The group played music and sang songs, and it turned out to be a real nice night and was repeated before the group left. The first party really broke the ice and from then on we were in the yards as much as the children.

At nights when everyone sat around chatting I would

borrow one of the group's piano squeezebox and I loved having a go at learning to play it, and a few days before they left Les gave me one that he had bought at a boot fair. I was really pleased with it and also I think it was really nice of him. I did learn to play Blue Spanish Eyes on it, well Willie taught me really, but I haven't played it for a long time now, it just don't seem right playing it indoors after being with the group learning to play, but I will start again someday.

Of a day time the children were learning to make lanterns and Les was making a Gypsy wagon. He did this really well and when it was finished my sister Liza helped him to paint it, and it looked really good, in one of the shows they used my husband's horse and Uncle Joe's cart and they put the wagon on the back, it looked really good when it was dropping in dusk and the parade came around the site, with the light from the lanterns the children had made. Before the group left they decided they would burn the wagon like Gypsies do when a relative has died, we all agreed that this would be a shame, so it was given to one of the children named Freddy. He had it for quite a while and the children used to play in it, then the bad storm came and it was destroyed which must have upset Freddy.

Apart from getting merry with drink from the parties, there was a chance to have a chat about the different ways that Gypsies have from *Gorjas* (non Gypsies). All in all it was a very relaxed and friendly atmosphere in the yards of an evenings, and speaking for the majority I would like it to happen again sometime.

Since the group have left all kinds of things have started to happen. Debbie came back to see us and through her we somehow ended up getting our own Committee together. The members were residents on our site, Jill, Uncle Dave, Uncle Siddy, Jimmy, Uncle Albert, Aunt Mary, my husband Terry, and Aunt Bubbles. Myself I don't know if having a committee can help us or not, but it was mentioned we should have one so we got together and formed one. I don't think they have many meetings now, but Aunt Bubbles still goes to different kinds of places and she has met all sorts of people. She has not long been back from Wales, where she met some Welsh Gypsies and also some important people who are trying to get education sorted out for Gypsy children. In fact I think the lady who she went to Wales with is one of the head people for the Save the Children organisation.

Some time ago now Bubbles was invited to go to a seminar up in London, also the children were asked to go to act out their circus play again. Chris (one of the students) came down to the site and picked the children up. Aunt Omey, Liza and me went with them. Once again we met the group and together with the children they all acted really well. One of the children whose name is Joe boy even hypnotised our council man. He asked him for some stables for our horses, a play area for our children and some fences for our plots. It never worked but Joe boy played the part well, and he shocked our council man who never knew it was going to happen. He bought all the children an ice cream after the show though and told them they had all done really well.

As I said, lots of things started to happen after the group left, and one of these things was Adult Education for Gypsies. Penny Roberts has started this up and she is trying to get some people together to teach Gypsies to read and write. I have joined this class that Penny runs and I enjoy it. I can read and write although my spelling is not that good, but at the moment I am learning to type. A couple of the women are learning how to use a sewing machine and another couple have tried typing. It's nice to know that even at an older age someone is willing to help you learn things you never thought you would get a chance to learn.

**Golia Anderson
Thistlebrook Caravan Site**

# Introduction

A low spread of caravans and mobile homes reaches
out as you reach Thistlebrook Caravan Site. Each tarmac 'pad' is
occupied in its own way, giving a powerful and concentrated individuality to each square. Members of an extended family sit on
their steps preparing food and chatting. Flowers hang in make-
shift bowls from fences, magnificent displays of Crown Derby
China cascade down inside the caravans. Men work over a lorry-
load in a workshop lit by welding light. Faces peer through trailer
windows at strangers: no secrets here. Everyone is both perfectly
friendly and slightly aloof. The same atmosphere of private pride
and public squalor that one meets in a ghetto .

Thistlebrook Caravan site is probably the largest official Travellers' site in Britain. It is situated in Abbey Wood, a
small Victorian suburb of East London with a large sixties council
estate on the south bank of the Thames. Abbey Wood found itself
dwarfed in the sixties when the new town of Thamesmead was
built on the marshes that stretch between Abbey Wood and the
Thames. These marshes were mostly associated with the
Travellers who for generations had stopped on them on their way
from the hopfields of Kent to the scrapyards of East London. A
number of Travellers stopped there regularly, some had settled
there and a number had bought plots of land. The floods of 1953
drove many of the Travelling families on the marsh to resettle in
the yards on the edge of Abbey Wood. When Thamesmead was
built both the yards and the land on the marsh were bought by

compulsory purchase and a portion of the old yards redeveloped and rented back to some of the local Travelling families in the form of a caravan site owned by Greenwich Council. Over fifty tarmaced enclosures with wash houses and electrical facilities make up the site where over 200 people live.

*Some of the current residents of Thistlebrook as children during the 1940s, photographed with a teacher, on Belvedere Marsh near where Thamesmead is today. Picture courtesy of Phyllis Grant.*

Thistlebrook residents pay a weekly site fee but do not have the same rights as other council tenants. They do not enjoy regular refuse collection or receive postal deliveries. Their children attend local schools, some have married non-travellers, some are awaiting transfers to council housing. Although few families spend much time travelling these days they strongly retain their culture and language which has survived despite the restrictions and pressures to conform.

Adjacent to the site is wasteground owned by Greenwich and Thamesmead Town. It is environmentally squalid, a magnet for fly tipping. With the aid of a few bulldozers it can be transformed into a temporary camp site, play area and open air theatre!

Emergency Exit Arts, formed in 1980, are a professional company of artists, performers and musicians. Based in South East London, we travel throughout the country and often work closely with local communities to produce spectacular celebratory events. In 1987 the site manager, John Gray, and the borough Arts Development Officer, Bradley Hemmings, invited us to explore the possibilities of taking an entertainment and arts in education programme onto the site. We have been working on

Thistlebrook since 1987. It has been our most rewarding and effective community based project.

The Travelling community was entirely new to us and Jon Cannon (also known as Jonky) and myself spent a few months getting to know more. We applied for funding, read up about Travellers, spoke to groups involved such as Teachers for Travellers and the Save the Children Fund, met local teachers and health workers and above all spent days knocking on trailer doors, chatting over fences and drinking endless cups of tea on Thistlebrook. Molly and Billy, my children, have become well known to the younger inhabitants of the site, breaking down barriers more straightforwardly than any Community Arts worker could hope to!

It became clear that many people on the site felt as suspicious and defensive about the outside world as outsiders often do about Travellers. There were young children and toddlers on the site who rarely left their mothers' sides; their mothers wanted to send them to playschemes and nurseries but were scared to leave them alone off the site. The community on the site seemed under pressure, a mobile, communal group had been forced into stasis and pushed too close together. Understandably, we were often greeted with suspicion. Even if what we suggested sounded good, no one believed it would actually happen. Eventually we had to take our hearts in our hands and go ahead anyway, very worried that we were imposing on a community that would rather be left alone. It was important to us to provide a service as we would with any community and not to patronise or interfere by 'doing good'. We could tell that this was a community that had learnt to expect nothing from the outside world and to act on the moment rather than make plans. We could never know for certain if our presence was helpful without trying it.

We decided that the most practical way to provide our service was to move onto the site ourselves. We find this an efficient way of remaining flexible to changing and uncertain needs, providing our own security and winning the mutual respect of the community around us while allaying any suspicions about our lifestyle and motives.

We first pulled on in August 1987. Council bulldozers flattened the ground. We pulled council caravans on to sleep in and put up a marquee equipped with everything necessary to provide a full two weeks playscheme. From the moment our marquee appeared Thistlebrook came to life. Young men appeared from nowhere to pull at guy ropes; we would never have got it up at all without the expert assistance of Joe 'The Colonel' Harris who barked instructions from the sidelines. The whole site responded with friendship, openness, trust – even gratitude: more children arrived every day and after a welcoming party at the end of our first week adults started coming down every evening to talk to each other and to us. This party was a watershed: almost the entire site came down and a dramatic lightning storm drove us all into the confined space of the marquee. Pushed together in this bright crowded space, as the rain beat down outside and the sky flashed, the atmosphere melted into an electric warmth and enjoyment. "The *Gorjas* in them houses are praying for it to rain on us" said 'The Colonel', "but they won't stop us having a good time!".". The place heaved with jiving figures, teenagers, married couples and people taking turns to sing into the microphone as the night drew on.

By the early hours a few Travellers and company members were left gathered round the fire, talking quietly and singing from time to time, our backs damp from midnight drizzle and our fronts warm with the bright fire. The first of many long and extraordinary conversations around fires as cultures and individuals met and discovered each other's hearts. The gathering round the fire of an evening was an important part of their social life that most of the people of Thistlebrook had done without since settling here. Before we knew it we were filling all the functions of a community centre, from citizens advice to entertainments. At the end of the fortnight the children put on a procession and a performance and we left quite overcome by the power of our experience amid all manner of affectionate goodbyes: the site clubbed together to buy us flowers and cards.

Before our arrival we built a spectacular procession with the children from the site and the local school and proceeded with our band 'Crocodile Style' through the site and the surrounding housing estate. From this point on it has been an important part of our work on the site to provide new bridges between the Travellers and the settled community. The Travellers of Thistlebrook now have a regular place in the yearly Woolwich carnival while the children have performed at national conferences on Traveller Site Management.

Since Summer 1987 we have returned to the site at regular intervals during the Easter and Summer school holidays. We continue to provide the basic services of a playscheme for children and a social centre for adults while attempting to build on this with new projects and possibilities. As an Arts Group our main aims are to focus on arts work on the site; producing progressively more ambitious performances with progressively greater involvement of children and adults. We hope to tour a short musical and shadow puppet show we wrote with the adults about the story of Thistlebrook around local Travellers' sites and schools.

As an outside group with the trust of the residents of Thistlebrook we have also been able to fill a valuable role as an intermediary and contact group for other bodies – health officers and adult education for example. It was at her first typing class that Golia wrote the piece which now serves as a foreword to this book. Not least we have been an excellent exercise in relations between the council and the site, being outside the 'official' world of 'the council' and at the same time a sign that the site is not forgotten and that things can be made to happen. New lines of communication have been set up, a tenants group formed, the environment of the site improved dramatically in recent months, through the efforts of John Gray the housing officer. His support throughout has been fundamental to our success. He is a rare housing officer who has the vision to encourage such a project. We see it as a measure of our success that the trust and support of the site has increased over the three years that we have been involved. Groups such as Adult Education, the London Bubble and Greenwich Council Play Department have become involved. One resident, our dear friend Bubbles Brazil, who gave us so much support from the very start, has become involved fighting for her people's rights, first in ACERT the education pressure group and now as a Travellers literacy worker employed by ILEA.

An important aspect of our work from the very beginning has been documentation of the project and oral work on the site. As both a writer and an outreach worker Jon has been an anchor in the community from the beginning. Wandering the site he consumes gallons of sugared tea and gets called over to perform to some visiting branch of the family his version of 'the Broomdasher', a song taught to him on the site, the title of which has become his nickname. As well as working on song lyrics and plots with children and adults on the site a diary of the entire project has been kept in words, documents and images. Days have been spent in trailers poring over family photograph albums and heirlooms.

All the quotations in this book were collected as part of this process: the conversations occurred spontaneously and were not recorded electronically but written down immediately after they took place. The trusting relationships we formed as a result of the project served to make the oral work particularly candid. Everyone quoted in the pages of this book has checked their

*15*

quotes and added to or altered them as they wish. We have tried to make the content of the book as relevant to the lives of all Travellers as possible; but as the book is rooted in one specific community of Travellers their voice and experience dominates. A few quotes are from Travellers in other parts of London: we felt it was important to include a few Irish voices. The first half of the book first appeared as a briefing for workers on our first site residency.

Another important aspect of documentation has been Renee Von's work with video which has resulted in a quality 20 minute video about the project being produced. We have also produced, with the Independent Photography Project of Woolwich an exhibition, 'Thistlebrook Travellers and Emergency Exit Arts'.

We do not regard ourselves as authorities on the subject but we do wish to share useful information and experiences, to tell a positive story and hopefully to encourage contact between communities. Hopefully this book can give the much-misunderstood lives of Travellers a wider voice.

Travellers have been isolated from the wider picture of community arts, educational and leisure provision. We have attempted to redress the balance and overturn some of the prejudices and hostilities that exist on all sides.

We all cherish memories of intense and exciting times spent on Thistlebrook, where we are known as 'the hippies' or 'the students': "We can't call you *Gorjas*, that'd be an insult."

**Debbie Mullins**
**Emergency Exit Arts**

# 1

## *i) People who travel*

### Travelling

People moved round the earth for thousands of years before they made fixed homes for themselves: in a sense, Travelling is the oldest way of life on earth.

As some people began to settle others remained on the road, continuing their ancient nomadism or servicing the settlements around them through fairs, markets or door to door. Isolated settlements needed to buy household odds and ends or have tools mended while landowners needed seasonal labour.

Today most people live in houses. Many of them move around in the course of their work; some choose to travel while others are forced to because of poverty or eviction.

Some take advantage of all these possibilities – and more – by living in caravans and moving around regularly. For these people, Travelling is a way of life. They are known as Travellers.

### Travellers

Their lifestyle makes Travellers conspicuous and thus easily persecuted. This can happen to anyone who takes up Travelling, simply because they live on the road. Many laws and regulations exist that can make this way of life difficult. Travellers can also be persecuted because of ethnic or racial prejudice.

Thus, Travelling is an issue of the human right to travel and to mobility, and it is also an issue of race, of cultural and ethnic rights.

The issues of prejudice and persecution have always dominated Travellers' lives and as a result of this their culture is

*19*

characterized by its strength, portability and adaptability in the face of oppression.

Travellers depend on the settled community for their livelihood and offer a variety of services that are best provided by living on the road. They support small industries within the settled community by investing money in china, trailers and other goods.

Travellers are some of the most disadvantaged and powerless, but proudest and most independent groups, of people in Britain today. Among the 30-50,000 Travellers in Britain there are three main communities: New Age Travellers, English Romany or Gypsy Travellers and Irish Travellers. There are also small communities of European Romanies.

The precise origins of the various groups of Travellers are unknown. Today's New Age Travellers have made a conscious decision to reject the conventional way of living. Romanies may ultimately be able to trace their origin to India, but the details of their history are unknown. Many Irish and Scottish Travellers took up Travelling after being dispossessed by landowners. It is possible that among Travellers are those who have their roots in nomadic cultures that never accepted or found admission to settled cultures. Some may have their origins in natural or human disasters or famines. Others simply saw an economic opening and filled it.

A person who lives on the road truly becomes a Traveller when they lose the aspiration to return to settled living and start to build a community and thus a culture around Travelling. As with any community, however, the boundaries are not clear. Anyone who lives on the road is a Traveller in the eyes of the law and can claim rights in defence of their lifestyle and culture, yet no one could ever call themselves 'Romany' or 'Gypsy' without having been born into that community; this is an ethnicity which has meaning quite independently of whether its members are Travelling or living in houses.

### Gypsy Travellers

Most English Travellers describe themselves as Gypsy or Romany Travellers. Gypsy Travellers in Britain have their own language, Romani, similar to that used by groups of Travellers throughout the world. Many of them feel that they belong to an international nation of Romany Travellers. Romany is the name they give themselves in this language.

Gypsy is an English word often used for Travellers, particularly Romanys. Some outsiders use it as an insult but many

Travellers are proud to call themselves Gypsy and feel a fierce pride in their identity and culture.

The Romani language has been traced back, through similarities of words and grammar to dialects from tenth century Sanskrit. There are Romany people using forms of this language in America, Australia and Africa, their ancestors having migrated to these places from Europe. Gypsies have migrated gradually. It is possible that they have their roots in India. The earliest definite written references to them are fourteenth century texts in Eastern Europe and the Near East.

People who travel

By 1600 every country in Europe had Travelling people, many of them being groups of Gypsy Travellers who had arrived in the last hundred years. Over the centuries these Travellers mixed with many peoples. Some gave up the travelling culture completely while some joined up with other Travellers. A powerful cultural inheritance has continued and today one often meets Gypsy Travellers whose physical features reach back to the Middle East and beyond. Romanys have avoided marriage outside their community and have remained a distinct ethnic group throughout their wanderings. The strength of this identity has tended to obscure our view of non-Romany Travellers in Britain, Europe and the Middle East. It is not known whether there are indigenous Travelling cultures in England as there are in Ireland and Scotland; certainly 'Tinker' has been recorded as a profession in England since the twelfth century.

*Irish Travellers*

Many Irish Travellers come from families that have travelled in Ireland for centuries. Stories of their past indicate that these families became dispossessed through the famines and other upheavals of Irish history, and subsequently many of these families have travelled in England just as English Gypsies have in Ireland. They have remained isolated from settled people both here and in Ireland for long enough to have their own dialect of Gaelic, called Shelta or Gammon. 'Tinker' is a word often used for them and other Travellers too. Its origin is 'metalworker' but it is often used as an insult.

The antipathy felt by some English Travellers and Irish Travellers is similar to the defensive attitude found in the settled community towards immigrants. This is despite the strong links and cultural similarities between English and Irish Travellers.

### New Age Travellers

New Age, or Hippy Travellers have made a conscious decision to reject the lifestyle of settled people and live on the road. Thus New Age Travellers are usually first generation and still have many connections with the settled world. Culturally their aspirations and values have more to do with the libertarian ideals of the late 1960s than the more traditional morality of other groups of Travellers.

This is the story of Travellers in England. Many aspects of their story and their way of life can easily be translated to other peoples and other places.

This book focuses on the experience of the Gypsy Travellers who played such a large part in its existence. We have tried to let other Travellers' voices speak wherever their experience is significantly different. In many ways they are very similar.

# ii) History

## Beginnings

In 1505 a group of people presented themselves to James IV of Scotland as exotic but faithful Christians fleeing heathen persecution. Their leader described himself as 'Lord of Little Egypt' and they were welcomed. This is the first that is known of Gypsies in the British Isles. These are the antecedents of British Romany Travellers. They had arrived from the continent, where similar encounters are recorded. Travellers' own stories explain their existence in an abstract, non-historical way while anthropologists have uncovered several possibilities[1].

The 'Egyptians' or 'Gypsies' as they came to be nicknamed are mentioned again a number of times over the next 40 or 50 years, fortune telling and dancing often attracting a favourable interest in them. Gradually, however, popular resentment and fear turned to persecution. In York for example there were mass killings of Gypsies. The law also reacted against them by ordering, in 1554, all 'Egyptians' to leave the country on pain of death; this death penalty was not repealed until 1783. It was difficult to establish for the purposes of the law who was and who was not an 'Egyptian'. What was a very distinct and foreign group in people's imaginations was not as easy to define in practice. Consequently, a law that was intended to attack a specific group of people became a persecution of all who travelled or seemed different. The law was extended by 1562 'for the avoiding of all doubts and ambiguities' to include:

> "all such sturdy and false vagabonds of that sort living upon the spoil of the simple people, in any company or fellowship of vagabonds, commonly called or calling themselves Egyptians or counterfeiting,

*transforming or disguising themselves by their apparel, speech or other behaviour."* [2]

By this time Travellers already filled a role in the economy and in people's lives. It was not easy to distinguish or separate the Gypsies from native itinerants and local peasants with whom they shared bonds more complex than simple enmity. This pattern has recurred in the history of Travellers in England. The Travelling culture in general and Romany culture in particular proved extraordinarily resilient and flexible and it continued to do so throughout the history of those who travel and those who want them to stop.

The Gypsies were one of our first immigrant communities and their experience over the centuries has been shared by many later ethnic groups and by Travellers all over the world.

What little else is known about Travellers before the nineteenth century is mainly drawn from literature and popular songs which portray familiar images of Gypsies as romantic, wild and carefree; wise and mysterious; dangerous outlaws. Those who got a more realistic and day to day impression of Travellers were by and large illiterate and unable to record their experience of Travellers' lives.

Similar attitudes and prejudices towards Travellers are to be found across the centuries. An eighteenth century writer talked of:

> *"Troupes of rogues, beggars, Aegiptians and idle persons"*, given to *"idleness and blind superstition."* [3]

While in 1830 another writer adds that they are:

> *"Vagabonds and itinerant tinkers, repairers of umbrellas and vagrants of the worst character."* [4]

While people accepted there was a group of Travellers they called 'Gypsies' they were uncertain who counted as a 'real' Traveller. Were these people vagrants, foreigners or something else? This confusion and suspicion is illustrated by such passages as that of 1610 where groups of people were described who:

> *"Goe alwais never under one hundred men and women, causing there faces to be made black, as if they were Egyptians."* [5]

If it was hard to identify Travellers in 1610, matters were no clearer two hundred years later:

> *"Vagrants of the worst character"* had *"lately found admission among the Gypsies, much lowered by such intermixtures."* [6]

Similar claims are often heard today. Those who were in contact with Gypsies as part of normal day to day life probably

_Travellers An Introduction_

held more positive attitudes towards them. A writer of 1832 felt they were:

> "*Considered useful by the peasantry and small farmers.*"[7]

Some Travellers in the eighteenth century found a place in history: such as Billy Marshall who became a folk-hero when he led a peasants' rebellion in Scotland; and the famous poet and radical, John Bunyan, who was a Tinker.

It is nevertheless quite likely that most Travellers – many of them descendants of sixteenth century 'Egyptians' – remained extremely poor and isolated. It is clear that many settled people were as scared and angered by their presence as they are today. Travellers survived this period in spite of the death penalty and have survived ever since.

**From the early nineteenth century to the last war**

By the late eighteenth century the development of industry was beginning to have an effect upon ordinary people's lives. Thousands of country people who had their land enclosed by big landowners moved to the new centres of industry in Britain's rapidly expanding towns and cities. This left many people landless and homeless. Perhaps some joined the 'vagabonds and tinkers, repairers of umbrellas and vagrants' described in 1830.

Some of the new kinds of work created had much in common with Travellers' lives, among them the travelling circuses which replaced the old fairs and the families who lived on the canals and worked the barges, sometimes still called 'water gypsies'.

The existing community of Travellers adapted to these changes and found they still had a role to play in the economy. Most importantly , improved road surfaces meant that Travellers could move with an ease and speed once unimagined. Previously Travellers had slept on the road in their carts or in 'benders tents': low tents made out of bent hazel branches and covered with material. Those with carts could now mount their benders on top and make them permanent. The familiar hoop-roofed Gypsy caravan was born. The richest of those Travellers who could afford a caravan turned them into the most magnificent travelling rooms. Only British Travellers have evolved such distinctive and decorative caravans and to this day a magnificent caravan is the badge and flag of the proud and successful Traveller.

Travellers moved from home to home offering such services as the mending and sharpening of tools, making and selling baskets, and dealing in such things as beehives or horses. Seasonal work was found in the country and casual work on the edges of cities, such as burning charcoal or sorting slag. There were many areas of waste or common land to stop on.

Travellers began to make more of an impression on literature and the writing of history. George Borrow became famous for writing books that depicted a romanticised version of his experience of Gypsy life. Hoyland, writing in 1816, paints a thumbnail sketch of Travellers' lives in south-east England at that time:

> *"A few of the Gypsys continue all the year round in London, expecting the attendance of fairs in the vicinity. Others, when work is scarce, go out twenty or thirty miles from the metropolis, carrying their implements with them on asses, and supporting themselves by the employment they obtain in the towns and villages through which they pass, and sometimes in haymaking, and plucking hops in the counties of Kent, Surrey and Sussex."* [8]

By the mid-twentieth century we can rely on remembered history and more is confidently known about Travellers' way of life. England's farms were busy producing food to feed the populations of the huge cities and were a major source of seasonal work, picking and harvesting. The dwindling number of common grounds and wastelands for stopping on were most easily found on the industrial fringes of cities while some employers offered temporary accommodation. Cities also brought work like fencing, tarmacing roads, railway and canal building and items such as clothes pegs and imitation flowers were sold door to door and fortunes occasionally read too.

Many Travellers came near the city for a winter base and moved further afield in the summer. Few travelled beyond a regular circuit of known sources of work within a few counties. Some still lived in benders and were lucky to afford a horse or cart. Wealthier Travellers owned or had rights to plots of land they could resort to as a base.

### Since the last war

The years since 1939 have seen more upheaval and change in the lives of Travellers than in any recorded time before. Many of the sources of work that Travellers have relied on for centuries have vanished, and the traditional foundations of the Travellers' economy have been threatened. Where and when

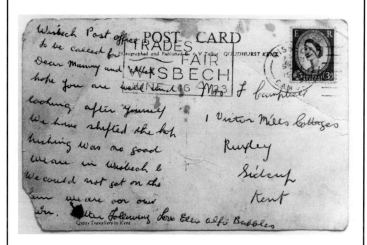

*Pictures courtesy of Bubbles Brazil*

Travellers stop has begun to be regulated by laws seriously restricting their ability to move. For the first time, the state has a systematic interest in the lives of Travellers.

Travellers were one of the groups singled out by the Nazis as 'racially impure'. 25,000 Gypsies died in the death camps.

The shock and bitterness caused by the war catalysed other motivating forces towards political organization among Travellers.

One of the most potent signs of this was the international development of Romany nationalism. In 1960 an International Romany Congress was held and, in 1971, the first World Romany Congress was held in London. In 1979 the United Nations recognised the Romany Nation and gave it representation.

The Gypsy council and other groups were formed during the 1960's in England. Travellers' rights became an issue of law and civil liberties, of education and social welfare. New laws and economic changes were destabilising Travellers' way of life and bringing them into the public eye and in conflict with the police.

The market for tinkering and for flowers and clothes pegs began to disappear during the 1960s. Fruit and vegetables were being mechanically picked and cheap, disposable plastic goods were easily available. With their traditional economy vanishing under their feet, Travellers were under great pressure to find new sources of work and scrap metal dealing became the main source of income for many Travellers.

Almost all Travellers have replaced their horse-drawn wagons with vehicle-drawn caravans and trailers. They have become more mobile and often more comfortable, but traditional stopping places continue to disappear. It is in making stopping more difficult that laws and governments have had their most oppressive effect.

> "Over centuries Gypsies have been persecuted in varying degrees but now a series of town and country planning, public health, local government, caravans and private acts and the bylaws they permit, has drastically reduced the number of stopping places available to them over a period of three to four decades." [9]

> "The Travellers subtly developed strategies for survival have been stripped from them by a whole series of post-war legislations that were never directly aimed at them." [10]

These developments undermined a basic freedom on

which Travellers depended, a right, according to the European Convention of Human Rights (Protocol 4 Article 2 Paragraph 1):

> *"Everyone lawfully within the territory of a state shall, within that territory, have the right to liberty of movement and freedom to choose his residence."* [11]

The more dislocated Travellers' lifestyle became, the more public their plight. The first council-built Travellers' site, a marker of the spiralling of need among Travellers, was built in Kent in 1960. Residents and politicians organised to oppose Travellers stopping in their neighbourhood. Evictions became more frequent and more fiercely contended. Anti-Traveller demonstrations like that in Tallaght, County Dublin, also made Travellers like Nan Joyce into popular heroines.

By 1968 the Government could no longer ignore the increasing tension being caused by shunting people from place to place. The Wilson Government passed legislation that dealt specifically with 'any person being a Gypsy'. The Caravan Sites Act (1968) asked every local council to provide at least 15 stopping places for Travellers. Any Council that did this (or could prove it had either no room for a site or no Travellers within its boundaries) could apply to the Department of the Environment for 'designation'. A designated borough could evict any other Travellers that appeared within its boundaries. A report by the Greater London Council says, this act:

> *"criminalises Travellers' ways of life over large areas of the country and gives councils the opportunity to make Travellers' lives absolutely unbearable."* [12]

The act sets no time limit on the building of sites, and no funds were provided for this until 1979. Councils have not hurried to provide them. One result of this has been to increase the instability of those living on the road. The Travelling community has come to be split between those who have somewhere secure to stop but are dissuaded from travelling for fear of losing it, and those who are on the road but are under constant threat of being moved on. One group can become ever more desperate while the other starts to lose its sense of identity.

Sites bring with them other complications: rules concerning travelling off the site, scrap breaking, or the lighting of fires can further undermine the Travellers' economy and lifestyle, while places can often go to those Travellers felt by local authorities to most legitimately deserve them, thus isolating other groups.

Although a number of parliamentary reports have drawn attention to the needs of Travellers little has been done –

'There are no votes in Travellers'. Even the small measure of protection from discrimination available through the Race Relations Act (1976) has often foundered over problems of defining an 'ethnic minority'.

New Age Travellers first made the headlines in the mid-1980s with the Peace Convoy. The virtual warfare declared on them by the government affected all Travellers. As Mrs Thatcher said: 'Anyone who makes life difficult for these people has my blessing'.

The Public Order Act (1986) Section 39 was a response to the issues raised by the peace convoy and relates particularly to Travellers. Any group of more than twelve vehicles can be moved by the police if the landlord is not happy with their presence and any group of less than twelve can be moved on if they cause 'damage' or 'nuisance'.

Some local authorities have tried to ease the problem by adopting non-harassment policies, or with other measures such as transit sites but these and the provision of too few official sites simply cannot deal with the problems faced by Travellers. One London family spoken to in 1987 said they had been moved on three times in five days. Conditions like this make eating, washing and sleeping hard, let alone making a living.

Attempts to legislate a solution to the needs of Travellers have been ineffective for reasons that echo down the centuries – an inability to identify the people and the problem the legislation is aimed at, and a lack of real will to deal with the situation. As a result legislation has created almost as many problems as it has solved. Yet the fundamental need, somewhere to stop, could be dealt with simply by building enough sites, as implied by the Caravan Sites Act (1968).

It is ironic that Travellers in many ways exemplify values held in high esteem today: making a lifestyle out of 'getting on their bikes', devoted to self employment and enterprise, upholding the family and traditional morality. Despite all this they have had to survive centuries of entrenched prejudice that continues to this day. On council land, squatting on roadside verges and empty spaces, given or rented space by landowners, on their own land, in council homes or in their own houses or bungalows, in mobile homes, caravans, wagons or benders, this isolated, divided, yet proud community is all around us.

Travellers
An Introduction

30

*The Smith family on Belvedere marsh during the
1940s. Picture courtesy of Phoebe King, née Smith.*

# iii) Culture

## Introduction

A Traveller's way of life revolves around varied forms of self-employment. Travelling and self employment are key elements in any Traveller's identity. In 1967, high court judges defined a 'gypsy' as:

> "a person leading a nomadic way of life with no fixed abode." [13]

The social anthropologist, Judith Okely, put it this way:

> "a self-reproducing ethnic group with an ideology of travelling and a preference for self-employment with a wide range of economic activities." [14]

Travellers make the definition much simpler:

> "we're Romanies because we roam."

The most fundamental features of Travellers' culture are practical responses to their way of life. This culture also serves to define Travellers in relation to the settled community.

The material for this book has been written and prepared with a group of English Travellers and it is from their culture that most of the material in this section is drawn. The differences between Irish and English Travellers' culture is very small and generally reflect the respective differences in the rural life of England and Ireland. Perhaps the Romanies' history of isolation through many cultures explains their particularly strong sense of identity and 'foreignness'.

Among New Age Travellers can be found all the sub-cultures of the last twenty years, particularly those that have their roots in the late 1960s. The details of Travellers' culture given in this section are far less applicable to them: it will be interesting to see if this changes as their culture ages.

## Travelling

Many Travellers say that travelling is a need they are born with. The patterns of travelling are those of work. Most follow a regular circuit through two or three counties, often wintering on the fringes of towns or cities and moving further out during the summer. Consequently the greatest concentration of Travellers is between the industry on London's edges and the farms of East Anglia and Kent that feed London. Most Travellers move as a family group or in small linked groups of families, though the dwindling number of stopping places often means there is no longer the security, or the peace, of choosing who you stop with. A few Travellers travel nationwide or even abroad.

## Isolation and identity

Travellers' isolation is partly due to poverty and oppression but it is also a source of pride and identity, serving to underline to Travellers the difference between themselves and the settled people with whom they must do business. There are Travellers for whom an outsider is as much a foreigner as Travellers are to many of us. The first, and often the only, Romani word settled people encounter is *Gorja*, also pronounced 'gowja', and means settled person or non-Traveller: sometimes with pejorative overtones. Travellers today mostly use their language, Romani, to communicate when outsiders should not understand, mixing Romani words and English grammar.

Travellers have always had to be adaptable sometimes hiding their identity whether to avoid attempts at genocide or simply to get the next job. At other times they have survived only because they have appeared exotic, attractive and entertaining. This experience increases the durability of their real identity which survives in portable, practical forms such as language, cleanliness beliefs and taboos, and the trailer.

The closest thing in a Travellers' world to a uniting, celebrating point for the community are at fairs, particularly that in Appleby in Cheshire during June.

## Men and women

As in most societies men are associated with work and women with the home. Friendly contact between unrelated men and women is very limited both before and after marriage. Couples may be members of close families known since childhood or they may be half-known to each other, through encounters at a fair or a stopping place, brought together as much to link two families as out of the love of two individuals. Matters of sex are rarely if ever discussed. It is not surprising to find such strong traditional attitudes to morality, sex and relationships in a community whose members have to live so close to each other.

The horse, once the essential animal of Travelling, is a passion among men as well as a source of income. The art of striking a good deal quickly is one of the essential skills of Travelling. Within the community, goods are swapped 'chopped' as much as they are bought and sold. Women also usually do door to door selling or 'calling' which requires a similar sharpness and perception. The most highly refined use of these skills is in the reading of palms (increasingly rare nowadays) where a quick and sensitive appraisal of a stranger and a way with words is necessary if it is to be successful.

Most Travellers agree that it is only in the last thirty or forty years that men have been the main breadwinners in Travelling families since formerly calling was relied on for day to day living.

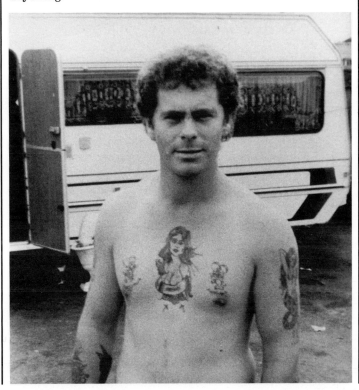

## Children and education

The boundaries between work and leisure, so clearly defined in the externally organized world of settled people, are blurred for most Travellers; as are the divisions between 'play' and 'work' and 'education'. Children are educated by experience and are encouraged to take on family responsibilities as soon as possible. By the ages of twelve or thirteen they have their own money and possessions and play a full part in the family.

Though on the whole most Travellers appreciate the value of literacy they tend to see exams and qualifications as unnecessary and irrelevant to their lifestyle, though these attitudes have changed as pressure on their traditional life has increased. Many Travellers feel they may need qualifications if only to be able to continue life on the road.

It is rare to find Travellers who are not determined to see their children getting primary education. This is often impossible when they have no secure stopping places or because they fear for their children in such an alien environment, or simply because local schools will not have them.

## The trailer and possessions

The trailer is home for most Travellers. Like a house the trailer and its contents are Travellers' most prized possessions and any money that can be spared will often be invested here. The trailer, its contents and mobility celebrates and exhibits many of the most important aspects of a Traveller's life: mobility, the family unit, cleanliness. It also acts as a portable investment. The mightiest trailers are custom built. With chrome plating and turquoise beading outside and cut glass mirrors and a baroque display of bowls and sideboards inside. A successful Traveller home may proudly display collections of Crown Derby and Royal Worcester china and of cut glass.

Many aspects of a Traveller's home are conspicuously laborious to keep clean and as such symbolise the high regard felt for cleanliness among Travellers within their space. The brightly arranged china plates and cushions have much in common with traditional English working class cultural tastes.

Features of a Traveller's world that can seem romantic to us are reminders of a culture that has disappeared since the war in most settled communities; good examples of this are the strong oral tradition, the close-knit community and the traditional morality (with all their advantages and disadvantages).

## Religion and beliefs

Religious beliefs vary as much among Travellers as they do among the settled people around them. Romany evangelical movements have won converts. Christening, white weddings and 'saying your prayers' continue to be important to many Travellers – as do superstitions of various origins. Few Travellers regularly attend church but religious feelings can run deep. Travellers in many parts of the world follow the dominant local religious beliefs, as well as having some of their own ways for some basic elements of life: rites of passage like marriage and funerals, taboos, cleanliness practices.

Travellers were traditionally married after a semi-serious mock elopement and where the boy and girl 'go off' together. Marriages nowadays are usually in church with a reception afterwards. Funerals are still quite different to the usual *Gorja* way. For several days the body lies in its caravan and all who knew the deceased come to pay their last respects. No expense is spared and elaborate shows of grief are common. Traditionally the trailer and all the belongings of the dead person are burned and places particularly favoured by them are avoided.

Travellers have strong feelings about cleanliness. Their practices are closely tied to the need to keep a clean family and food while living on the road. Separate bowls are kept to divide the washing of food and cutlery from that of the clothes and the body; if the bowls are mixed up or touch something else unclean they are felt to be polluted and are destroyed. Similar beliefs can be found in nomadic societies and other societies that do not rely on household machinery as much as we now do.

The social anthropologist Judith Okely felt that at their most abstract and unconscious level these beliefs about cleanliness can be seen to symbolise a complete world view, dividing clean from unclean. Only clean things can go inside the body; while the clothes and skin outside can be dirtied, so the two must not come in contact with each other. Thus are divided clean from unclean; inside the body from outside the body; inside the trailer from outside the trailer; living from dead and within the community from outside the community. It is in feelings like this that a sense of identity is most clearly underlined; nurturing, validating and maintaining the strength of a group of people who depend for survival on dealing in isolation with others who persistently mistreat them.

## Power and organisation

Travellers have relied for centuries on being amorphous. There is no formal power structure or tradition of group organisation. Individuality and flexibility are felt to be important. 'Never make plans'.

There are greatly differing degrees of wealth and influence among Travellers. Although there are always alliances and conflicts between families and groups of families, there are no organisations or leaders as we understand them. This amorphousness has been a source of considerable frustration to other people whether they want to support or to oppose Travellers. The impossibility of pinning down who or what Travellers are has always been their greatest strength and their greatest weakness. With no fixed system of authority it has been impossible to attack them as a group, each family or group finding its own answers to new difficulties while remaining within the vague framework of travelling and self-employment. Conversely it has also made it easier for those in power to discriminate against Travellers without meeting organised resistance.

This flexibility has made it possible for groups of Travellers to preserve for hundreds of years a language and a culture quite separate from those found in the settled world. The price of this flexibility has been to keep them one of the most maligned and isolated groups in England. It has been said by some Travellers that they form a doorstep 'third world' class of people, playing a part in the economy but kept apart from others in it.

The upheavals of the last thirty years have been considerable but while there has been an economic niche for Travellers – "The occasional supply of goods, service and labour, where demand and supply are irregular"[15] – governments have been unable to stop people travelling. Travelling fulfils basic functions in society. It will change as it has always done and it will survive as it always has done – with difficulty and with pride.

In some ways Travellers are at the bottom rung of opportunity in our society, in other ways this isolated, divided, yet proud community is one of its most flexible and independent groups.

Culture

# 2

## *by the Travellers of Thistlebrook and elsewhere*

### Travelling people

Travelling people think differently to other people. Freedom, like.
They don't like having rules put on them.

*Mickeen McCarthy,*
*Hackney*

A Travelling Man is a gifted man. He can do anything.

*Mickeen McCarthy*

We're Romanies because we roam.

*Common saying*

If we've got no money we grab a basket and go out and get it.

*Cindy Harris,*
*Thistlebrook*

### Where we come from

Travellers come from all over. Everywhere. Once everyone lived
in tents. Travellers just never went into houses when everyone
else did. They wanted to keep their freedom.

*Marion Mahoney,*
*Bow*

No-one knows where we really come from. They can make suppo-
sitions but that's all it is, supposition. I think it's from India. Some
say Egypt, some say all over.

They used to say we was searching for the missing nail. We was asked to make nails for the crucified Christ, or we lost one. The old ones used to say it: we're searching for the missing nail – that's why we're travelling.

*Bubbles Brazil,*
*Thistlebrook*

They say our language is based on Indian, like if you speak to an Indian in Romani he'll understand a lot of what you say, and it's got lots of other languages in it from all the other countries we've come from.

*Bubbles Brazil*

It's our language. It's the Indians talk, our talk, the black man's talk, Gypsies' talk. If you go to India he'll understand what you say.

*Betsy Scamp,*
*Thistlebrook*

It's only *Gorjas* that say we come from India. When we first come to Europe we said we were from Egypt. We could've come from all different places. I don't think so though. Wherever you go in Europe, Gypsies look the same.

by the Travellers of Thistlebrook and elsewhere

We're the only nation on Earth that don't know where their natural born home is, but we must have come from one place.

*Bubbles Brazil*

"They should make us a country, like they did the Jews".

"Then you'd have to stop travelling, to grow food, or open a shop".

"No-one'd do that!"

"You'd go to see the King and he'd have gone off hop-picking!"

"Everyone would want to be King anyway!"

"They'd have to move the capital every day!"

"You couldn't give us a country because we needs *Gorjas*. We couldn't be Travellers without them. We survives off them!"

"We'll always be a scattered nation. There'd be no Travellers without *Gorjas*".

"And there'd be no *Gorjas* without Travellers!"

*Joe Smith, Primrose Brazil, Bubbles Brazil,*
*Thistlebrook*

### "We've got different ideas"

It's when the spring comes you've got to go. You've got to. It's coursing through your veins, telling you. Soon as spring arrives you've got to go.

*Bubbles Brazil*

# The Broomdasher

There was a nasty Broomdasher
Shabbing through the crack
With his bands and his peters and his bottoms on his back.
He came upon the Yogger
He stamped and then he swore:
"Believe me Mr Yogger, I've never been here before"

The Broomdasher rised up on his feet
And he poggered him, nice and neat.
Away went the Broomdasher, shabbing for his life!
There was a farmer in a field, and he hollered to his wife:
"There goes a starvation Broomdasher, shabbing for his life!"

*'Major' Jones*
*Alfred Brazil*
*Thistlebrook*

Broomdasher = Poacher
Shabbing = Running
crack = wood
bands, peters, bottoms = traps
Yogger = Gun/Gamekeeper
poggered = beaten

I was away last year, right from the start of the year right to the late of the year. Doing a bit of work, work as you go. Do roofing, painting, anything you can earn a shilling at, garden digging, anything. I s'pose you'd do a little bit of dancing if it came to it! Long as you was earning a day's work.

*Albert Moore,*
*Thistlebrook*

A few of us deal horses. But most of us like to keep 'em – like a hobby. You'd never see us without 'em. We used to keep 'em to pull our wagons but now we just keep 'em. My dad always had one, I've had one since I was a kid and my kid'll have one soon as he's old enough. We'd go insane without 'em . . . Sometimes I go to the field just to watch him eating. I'll fall asleep watching him and he'll eat all round me.

*Terry Anderson,*
*Thistlebrook*

The men deal a little scrap and we go out calling. Selling flowers and household bits and pieces and reading fortunes. When you've been in so many houses you can tell in ten minutes what class of man you're talking to and how his parents brung him up. You go with your friend or with your kids to learn 'em. Going from door to door or selling heather in the street.

*A Traveller,*
*Thistlebrook*

*Gorja* kids all keep themselves to themselves where as our kids will share anything – but they don't get independent till much later. When we goes calling our kids keep what they earn.

*Bubbles Brazil*

A Travelling man doesn't believe in banks. You can see if he's wealthy from the silver, chrome, china and glass. You can tell us by what we carry.

*Marion Mahoney*

We've got different ideas what's clean. I think its cleaner as long as it's away from the trailer. The trailer's always clean . . . moving around all the time I suppose you think differently. And we don't get no rubbish men!

*Bubbles Brazil*

You may see rubbish outside people's trailers but they're always clean inside. We use them chrome pots. Some of them may cost a hundred pounds each but they last a lifetime. We keep them separate. I wash vegetables in one, clothes in another, dishes in a third. Settled people don't do that. You won't find a Travelling person who doesn't.

*Marion Mahoney*

We've got to be cleaner than *Gorjas* ain't we. If you mix up your bowls it's got to be filth hasn't it. It doesn't make sense to me. There's got to be germs.

*Bubbles Brazil*

If a girl was courting a boy she had to do it in secret, just to meet up and talk. I think the parents was frightened to lose the child. When they was ready, they'd go away together. If they stopped a night out on their own, 9 times out of 10 the parents wouldn't have her back. That was it. We didn't do marriage like you do.

*Betsy Scamp*

48

We still burn the caravans sometimes. All take one thing out each, and then you burn it. That way you know where everything is. That way there's no worries.

It's probably so you don't have to carry anything round with you.

And we always bring a body home when he's dead and sit up with him for so many days and so many nights, in his trailer. Well it's only right.

He lived there all his life so you've got to bring him to his place when he dies, it's only right. We wouldn't go back there after he died.

*Bubbles Brazil*

by the Travellers of Thistlebrook and elsewhere

When someone dies, we sit up with them for four or five nights. At the funeral everyone sends a big wreath, perhaps of something they owned or liked which had a connection with themselves, if you know what I mean. We burn their trailer afterwards and we wear black for a year or two as well.

*Golia Anderson,*
*Thistlebrook*

### "I'm Proud to be a Gypsy"

There is something there that's different. You don't know what it is, you only know it's there if you've been with us, or if you are one. You couldn't never put no words to it, . . . It's something to be proud of . . . I'm proud I'm a Gypsy.

*John Harris,*
*Thistlebrook*

There's other Travelling people and all Travelling people have the same rights. But nobody else can call themselves Gypsy, that's not right. We were born to this way of life, it's our birthright. We've been like this for hundreds of years.

*Bubbles Brazil*

Mind you there's probably not a single pure bred Gypsy anywhere. It only takes one of your sort of people.

*John Harris*

I'm not just a Travelling person, I'm a Romany. There's plenty of *Gorja* Travellers. I've met a few of them and they're a pitiful sight! And then there's them Hippies. If there were more people like them there'd be no problems. And there's the Irish. But I'm a

49

Gypsy, a Romany, and I'm proud of it

They're nice people them Hippies. We stopped with them once. Real ones they was, with their wigwam and their coaches and their convoy. It blew up a gust and the wigwam went right over!

More people like that and there'd be less trouble in the world. If everyone was like them there'd be no fighting . . . but people hates 'em, don't they.

*Bubbles Brazil*

"The Irish Travellers have only been coming over here for the last ten or twenty years. There wasn't hardly any of them before that."
"They're only in the same boat as you. We only say about them what others say about us."
"But we're English."
"Look at Gran, she wasn't English. Her people had copper-coloured skin, like a red Indian. They weren't English."

*Bubbles and Moses Brazil*

The English Travellers make out we're taking the bread out of their mouths. If they was in Ireland we'd probably be the same.

*Marion Mahoney*

The Irish have been Travelling for hundreds of years too, and they've got their own way of speaking, but we can't understand it. I don't know why, I suppose they're not our tribe.

*'Colonel' Joe Harris,*
*Thistlebrook*

They're lovely people. Their watering cans glitter. Their motors are nice, trailers are nice.

*Albert Moore,*
*Thistlebrook*

If you did have a Travelling MP he'd have to answer for all the Travellers not just some . . . if you don't help them all, you don't help none of them – they're all Travellers.

*Bubbles Brazil*

All Travellers are one. I don't believe what they say about the differences between them.

*Moses Brazil*

We're all Travellers. Everybody's equal.

*Bubbles and Primrose Brazil*

**Gorjas**

I don't think I'm better than anyone – but I think I'm just as good. I treat everyone the same, no matter what they are.

*Gorjas* aren't like that. They sort of divides people up. They treats them different like. And I don't think they like us because we don't.

*Bubbles and Elly Brazil*

When they're young, they hear about Gypsies stealing babies and bringing them up, baby talk like that . . . It's either that or it's the fiddle playing man with the necktie . . . They forgets it of course when they're older but it sticks somewhere deep inside.

*John Harris*

If one of them in Thamesmead nicked something from here we'd say oh, it's him in number 15 or whatever. But if one of us nicks from them it's oh, it's them gypsies again.

*Traveller, Thistlebrook*

All they ever want to do is move you on.　　*Traveller*

Them lot over there in them houses. They love it when it rains. They're all sitting there praying for it to rain on us.

*'Colonel' Joe Harris*

Look at them over there. You can't tell me they're happy in them (estates) can you? All closed in on top of each other there. They're just piles of boxes. That's why you get all them suicides and break-downs. It's terrible, it would drive you out of your mind in one of them. It would send them all crazy, I don't know how they stand it.

*'Bubbles' Brazil*

If you ever lived in a house you'd be lonely – never see who's next door . . . you'd be frit there's murders downstairs while you're asleep upstairs. I'd never sleep upstairs. It'd be lonely and danger-ous in a house. When Travellers started going into houses some of the old ones died of it. They couldn't stand it. Great Nan pitched her tent in her front room! 'Houses are alright' she said, 'but they've got them terrible walls!'.

*'Bubbles' Brazil*

by the Travellers of Thistlebrook and elsewhere

*51*

## "In the old days"

I love Travelling. You'd sleep somewhere in the sun . . . for the winter we used to have four horses, a wagon . . . and a trolley, that was his hawking trolley. When the summer come he'd leave the wagon and a van in the back of a pub . . . where they know you. We'd get along down to the pear country and cut some sticks, bend 'em over and we'd have a wagon, a tilter . . . we used to lay under it, and mum and dad and the smallest children on top or in a bender tent. It was lovely in the summer, it didn't matter where you lay, 'cos it was lovely, all you wanted in the summer was a couple of blankets, something to keep the rain off and the wind out.

*Betsy Scamp*

Oh, you stop in some right pretty places. You think back and you only remember the good times! That summer when you stopped in a green lane or field and no one troubled you and it was a dear little pretty place to be stopping. Not the winter when you were moved on three times in one day, or woken at seven in the morning with a rat-a-tat on the window and the *gavvers* (police) want you to get out in the blinding snow and they won't let you have a cup of tea; when they're waiting for you at the next place, and you're glad to stop in knee deep snow by the road if it's a place you won't be moved on.

*'Bubbles' Brazil*

"The only bit of a holiday you had was when you went hopping."
"And that was work."
"A Traveller only knowed a working holiday. Farming. Hopping, 'taters, cherry picking."

*Albert and Mary Moore*

Spud bashing is the hardest work among field work. You've got to pick 'em that quick before the spinner comes back again, and oh, mate, your back!

*Betsy Scamp*

In the old days Travellers didn't have no choice. They just ate what they could get. Which is why they had their dogs, greyhounds: to get rabbits, hares.

*Siddy Hildon,*
*Thistlebrook*

by the Travellers
of Thistlebrook
and elsewhere

There was times you wouldn't get your next meal until you'd gone calling for it.

*Betsy Scamp*

You grew up with no social, no family allowance, no job. How could you stay alive? . . . Things were very hard. Everyone worked when you could get it, picking in the summer. In the winter there was nothing. The men would go and find food. The women would go hawking, calling.

Clothes pegs, baskets, lace . . . pegs go best – people always needs 'em – pegs and line props. Baskets go well at Easter time, for the primroses, elderwood flowers at Christmas.

*Betsy Scamp*

The men never used to do any work, making a few pegs and flowers, but just sitting round the fire and talking. The women did it all. That's changed now, but before the war it was all like that.

*Bubbles Brazil*

Women going out with baskets and getting a living. That's how it used to be, years ago and once upon a time, the women used to go out and get the grub, and the men used to take the vans along, it was horse time, you know. The wagon and the horse. They got water, wood . . . it was different to what it is today.

*Albert Moore*

The mother was the breadwinner.

*Betsy Scamp*

Scrapping only started with scrapyards – and having sites to put scrap on. You used to get next to nothing for a ton of scrap.

*Moses Brazil*

We were always taught – never tell them who you are. You can get things now sometimes if you say you're a Traveller but you couldn't get nothing then.

*Bubbles Brazil*

You never went to school because you never had time. Soon as you pulled in you'd be pulled out.

*Mary Moore, Thistlebrook*

You had to put your name and 'No Fixed Abode' on any wheeled vehicle or you'd be summonsed. You'd be moved on anyways,

by the Travellers
of Thistlebrook
and elsewhere

*1950s. Picture courtesy of Bubbles Brazil.*

your kids could be taken. You'd be done because you were too close to the road or you'd damaged the hedgerow. You'd be fined for everything. Every time you stopped a policeman come and took your name, date of birth, where you just come from.

*Bubbles Brazil*

55

### "You've got to change"

Things have changed. It was around 1959 things changed. Travellers were always country people. That's how you think of them, isn't it, country people. Never went near towns. I hated towns, Travellers have a natural aversion to them, I think so. We never started coming up to them till then. And all the real Gypsies, northern Gypsies; They're still country people. But you had to go near the town – you had to. All the country work went. All the farms where we always used to stop, started getting machines and big fields. So we had to do more scrapping.

But we always done some scrapping. Gypsies has always done scrapping work, always. I reckon every Traveller has done a bit at some time in his life.

Calling's changed and all. You can still make pegs and carnations from elderflower and swag, but if you charge for the time it took you, who'll buy it? They can get clothes pegs for 20p down the supermarket, and silk flowers in the corner shop.

Everyone's started getting motors – well you had to, didn't you? That's what I mean when I say times have changed – everything's got faster. Everyone's wanting more and more. Everyone's got motors, and then you need bigger pads and you wouldn't want to go as slow as a wagon. You couldn't drive a wagon down the M4 with four horses behind! And all the horses now are silky little beauties, 'cos no-one needs 'em for work. In the old days the pace was slow, no-one hurried for anything. Now you have to go faster and faster, everyone's all trying to keep up with everyone else.

You got these sites, and they changed people. You got to change, Travellers have always had to change. Things began to get better in the sixties, but now they're much worse again. They fetched in all these new laws. It's better now to be on a site, but you lose your identity.

*Bubbles Brazil*

This is what's done it now, the old big trailers. This is a house, there's no good saying it ain't, it's a bungalow. It's very *Gorjafied* isn't it. Only thing is we've got a bit of Crown Derby, with a little bit of brass, what keeps you back as a Traveller. Other than that it's just square one, isn't it. Where do you hear a generator going today. It's unnatural.

There's a lot come from the houses and settled in, just married in and it's gone the other way with 'em. They like our sort of life better than they do your sort of life. That's what it seems like. It's as they say: 'everybody wants to be a Traveller, but nobody wants to be a *Gorja*'.

You've never been a Traveller, you either are a Traveller or you're not. You've probably Travelled more than anybody on this site. You might as well say you're a Traveller!

Nine out of ten of them's what I call Plastic Gypsies. All they want to do is live on a site.

*Albert Moore*

by the Travellers of Thistlebrook and elsewhere

You've got to change, but it's terrible. It's not so hard now as it was, but then you made your living by being what you were. Now you make a living by hiding it and you have to hide it.

You've got to be more *Gorjafied*, and we needs education, but it's a terrible thing because in 20 years time there won't be any more Travellers on the road anymore.

*Bubbles Brazil*

We wouldn't have changed if we didn't have to. It's only *Gorjas* that's made us change, and the ones that don't want to be Travellers no more, apart from that we would be. They've got you in a corner and you've got to change.

*Cindy Harris*

The old ones are used to fire and scared of electricity: the young ones can't light a fire but they know everything about electricity.

*Traveller*

We young ones have got to change, but the old ones they can't. They can cope with no electricity because they been used to it, but we've been brought up with it. The old saying is: what you've never had, you'll never miss. Young or old, once you've had something, you get used to it.

*Cindy Harris*

Years ago you never heard of people marrying out – but he's got a *Gorja* wife and I've got a Gypsy husband and you both got to change a bit.

*Traveller*

All the Travellers knowed was farm work. Land – strawberry, apple, carrot topping . . . But the younger generation what do they do – tarmacing, roofing, building. In years to come there'll be many Travelling people but there won't be real Travellers.

*Cindy Harris*

*Courtesy of Henry King 1920s*

I was right in the changing. I've been half me life with the old ones and half my life with the new. I prefer the old ones. Their principles was better. I don't think they'd've liked to accept social security. You had to in the end, but they wouldn't've liked it. They sort of shared what they had though. When they was hard up they was more happier.

*Betsy Scamp*

## Sites and stopping places

It's the sites that are killing them. They shouldn't have put them here, it's destroying our way of life. These government sites, they stop you Travelling and they try to make you live different. All the younger ones don't cook outside, they're not real Gypsies. That's why they don't travel anymore. They listen to pop music, go to schools. They should never have started it, they're destroying our ways. Some of the young 'uns – and there's only a few of us old ones left – if you pulled them off here and sent them off and they didn't know they had a place on another site somewhere – they wouldn't know what to do on the roadside. They're not really Gypsies, anymore.

*'Colonel' Joe Harris*

All the stopping places Travellers had for years are all closed up. All the old commons that we used to stop on when I was a child have got bye-laws on them. All the lanes, 'The Romany Roads', as we used to call them.

*Traveller,*
*Belvedere*

Travellers were never allowed to own their own land – they never got permission . . . so they put us all in sites, like they did the Indians in America, in reservations, to get rid of us.

*Siddy and Peggy Lee,*
*Thistlebrook*

We trusted governments and councils in them days but we never got anything.

*Terry Anderson,*
*Thistlebrook*

*59*

You can only compare us to the Red Indians in America – they put you in a reservation. Everything that's part of a Gypsies heritage they say we can't have. It's to stop us from Travelling and to stop us doing half the things we were used to. People in houses with no bath and an outside loo get on the news!

*Cindy Harris*

*Picture courtesy of Cindy Harris*

When you pull off a site, the longing kind of leaves you and you want to come back to your comfort. On the official sites they want to show you how to live.

They won't let him put scrap on his plot. That's how we earn our living that sort of thing – we don't want it there but we have to have it there. It's our living . . .

*Traveller,*
*Thistlebrook*

I know it's harder on the road but sites is the worst thing what's ever happened to Travellers. Travellers weren't made to be penned in like that. Everything goes right out of you. It's ruining Travellers, it's killing 'em.

*Bubbles Brazil*

# Thistlebrook Rap

I was walking through the site
Late one night
When Alf jumped out
And guv me a terrible fright

by the Travellers
of Thistlebrook
and elsewhere

It was a sight
That Saturday night
It made me shout
And jump about
(I didn't half give him an earful!)

Then he staggered to one side
So I thought I'd run and hide
So I went down to the pub

I come staggering out
And gave my mum a fright
So I thought I'd run and hide

Because my mother had already found Alf

Lying in a skip
With a smile on his lips
Looking for something to drink

So along came my mother
Said 'Get home, my brother –
'Cos your sister's just had a fit!'

I went home to see her
She said that I bit her
And she hit me with a slipper
And said 'I'm no quitter
Pass me the bitter!'

*Primrose Brazil*

Primrose wrote this rap about a Saturday night with Emergency
Exit Arts and subsequently performed it at parties.

They want the place to look like Butlins but it's not Butlins, we're not on holiday, it's our way of life.

*Moses Brazil*

People are just glad to have a stopping place – you can't live on the roads no more.

*Cindy Harris*

It's not perfect on here but we've all got our places and some hard standing. It's the ones that are still on the road that need the help.

*Bubbles Brazil*

They get pushed from pillar to post and when they see a caravan they stop by it.

*Traveller,*
*Thistlebrook*

There's people out there you wouldn't believe. People living in benders in the woods. People who wouldn't understand you if you spoke to 'em.

*Traveller,*
*Thistlebrook*

Of all the families we've stopped with over the last 20 years – maybe 500 families – there's only four still on the road all year, Travelling.

*Bubbles Brazil*

I don't know about the young ones but I miss the old days. But I always say, once your wings are gone, you're finished.

*Albert Moore*

#### "We're the bottom of the pile"

You can't put up a sign saying 'No Black People' or you'll be done good and proper. But it's 'No Travellers' or 'van people' all over. I tell you we're the bottom of the pile. We ain't got nothing.

*Terry Anderson*

They thought we all had polio . . . they used to come down at night with petrol bombs and air-guns.

*Marion Mahoney*

If people know we're Travellers, we don't get the job.

*Bow site*

It's like everything else, isn't it. A Traveller's back is broad.

*Albert Moore*

I'm only a poor old Gypsy man, and when I'm dead and gone, They'll burn me trailer, bury me body, and tell me I've moved on.

*'Colonel' Joe Harris*

by the Travellers of Thistlebrook and elsewhere

People don't mind Gypsies if they look pretty. They like them with horses and wagons and not with trailers, motors and scrap.

*Bubbles Brazil*

They all end up together in one area, all the Gypsies in England, in one clump, and they'll have to put a bomb between them if they want to separate them.

*Traveller, Belvedere*

**Times to come**

I'll tell you what the problem is! I'll tell you why we've always been treated like bloody beggars and killed and abused! Because we haven't got any leaders! Look at the unions! If the farmers in France all decided to sell cheaper than the farmers in England, they'd all be out on the streets with everyone behind them and they'd block the streets until it was stopped. That's what we should have had . . . maybe in the past we got by because we didn't have leaders, but whether we needed them in the past, or not, we need them now.

*'Colonel' Joe Harris*

Never make plans dear, you must never make plans.

*Common saying*

I tell you what, we've always been able to change, we'll always take up something new when it comes up – take whatever's going all the way through life. You have to be able to take what's going in this life.

*63*

*Moses Brazil*

Life's hard nowadays. Soon it'll all be computers and robots. But they'll always need plates, won't they. No matter where they put them there'll still be Travellers. They'll not change their way of life because they've gone into flats. There'll be a trailer outside and horses outside the door. You'll know they're Travellers. It'll look like a caravan.

*Marion Mahoney*

# Further Reading

*Gypsies*, Thomas Acton, Macdonald, 1981.
    Mainly on Romany Travellers but very good for school use.

*The Traveller's Handbook*, an introduction to Travellers and the Law. Bill Forrester, Interchange Books, 1985.

*Traveller – an autobiography*, Nan Joyce, Gill and MacMillan, 1985.
    An excellent and moving book. Nan Joyce, a Traveller, rose to prominence in the sixties in Ireland in her fight for Travellers' rights.

*Gypsies – An Illustrated History*, Jean-Pierre Liegeois, Al Saqi Books, 1983.
    Also excellent, with a global perspective on Romany culture in particular.

*Changing Cultures – The Traveller-Gypsies*, Judith Okely, Cambridge, 1983.
    A fascinating social-anthropological study of a group of English Travellers.

*A Traveller Child*, Jose Patterson, Hamish Hamilton, 1986 (for children).

*Roma: Europe's Gypsies*, Grattan Puxon, Minority Rights Group, 1987.

*Gypsy Family*, Mary Waterson, A&C Black, 1978 (for children).

*The Yellow on the Broom*, Betsy Whyte, Futura, 1986.

*Travellers from the Stars*, ILEA Teachers for Travellers, 1989 (for children).

*The Education of Travellers in Inner London*, ILEA Teachers For Travellers, 1989.

*Moving On*, Minority Rights Group, 1987.

*Profile on Prejudice*, Minority Rights Group, 1985.

Most of these books include longer bibliographies and resources' information. There is a lot of material around but it is on a small scale and quite scattered and much of it ignores non-Romany Travellers. Some of the best material has been produced by locally based teachers and activists so it is worth searching them out. London's Teachers For Travellers and Bradford's Education Service for Travelling People both have produced children's books and booklets about and for Travellers.

| Teachers for Travellers, | Education Service for Travelling |
|---|---|
| c/o Ilderton School, | People |
| Varcoe Road, | Fairfax School, |
| London SE16 3LA. | Flockton Road, |
| | Bradford, BD4 7RJ. |

Such groups may also have videos and exhibitions, for example:

*Stopping In London*
Travellers Video Project, 26 Powis Square, London W11 2AZ.

Emergency Exit Arts' Video "And a good time was had by all" and Exhibition about our Travellers project and Thistlebrook, available from:

Debbie Mullins, Emergency Exit Arts, PO Box 570, Deptford, London, SE8 3HL.

# *Resources*

There are a range of voluntary bodies concerned with Travellers, some set up by Travellers themselves.

ACERT (Advisory Committee for the Education of Romany and other Travellers), Keepers High Wych, Sawbridgeworth, Hertfordshire.

British Rommani Union, Hever Road, Edenbridge, Kent, TH8 5DJ.

Minority Rights Group, 29 Craven Street, London, WC2N 5NT.

National Association of Teachers for Travellers, Broad Lanes, Wolverhampton.

National Gypsy Council, Greenhills Caravan Site, Greengate Street, Oldham, Manchester, OL4 1DG.

National Gypsy Education Council, 32 Marshall Road, Steering, Colchester, Essex, CO5 9LQ.

Many local authorities have teams of teachers for local Travellers, official sites with site wardens, Travellers' workers or working parties. They are worth contacting to find out about Travellers in your area. They will also be able to put you in touch with your local Travellers' Support Group or Irish community support groups, if either exist.

National bodies who have contact with Travellers include:

Commission for Racial Equality, Elliot House, 10-12 Allington Street, London, SW1 5EH.

Department of Education and Science, Arthur Ivatts, HMI for Traveller Education, Portcullis House, Seymour Grove, Old Trafford, Manchester, M16 ODJ.

National Council for Civil Liberties, 21 Tabard Street, London, SE1 4LA.

Save the Children Fund, Travellers section, Mary Datchelor House, 17 Grove Lane, Camberwell, London, SE5 8RD.

# Acknowledgements

We are very grateful to the Greater London Arts Association for their generous grant which paid for the printing of this book.

Also to the London Borough of Greenwich for their funding of the Travellers project. Particularly the Play, Housing, and Arts Officers. The project was also funded by Greater London Arts. Special thanks to John Gray (Housing) and Bradley Hemmings (Arts) for their constant financial and practical support, and to The Independent Photography Project (TIPP), Woolwich for all their help. Thanks to the two Debbies. All photographs are by Jon Cannon and printed by Sarah Wyld of TIPP. Cover photo printed by Anne McNeill of the Montefiore Community Education Centre.

And thanks to all those who have worked with us on Thistlebrook:

Rose Ablett
Janie Andrews
Kate Barfield
Geoff 'Pecker' Bowyer
Circus Bumbelini
Clarissa Brown
Nick Catermole
Will Embling
Kate France
Jo Green
Mark Gregg
Collette Hannon
Dave Hitchen
Lalo
Gavin Lewery

Chris Lurca
Sam and Graham Morton Parker
Debbie Mullins
Les Sharpe
Greg Stevens
Debbie Swallow
TIPP
Alice Power
Mary Robson
Carolyn Roy
Renee Von
Chris Wolverson
Beccy Wright
and all the members of 'Crocodile Style',
and to all the Travellers of Thistlebrook: particularly the Andersons, Brazils, Hildons, Moores, and Orpwoods.

# References

1 Jean-Pierre Liegeois' book *Gypsies* has more material on the origins of Romany and other Travellers.

2 Okely, *The Traveller-Gypsies*, p3 Judith Okely Cambridge 1983.

3 Okely p3.

4 *ibid* p6.

5 *ibid* p3.

6 *ibid* p6.

7 *ibid* p6.

8 *ibid* p126.

9 *Cripps Report*, HMSO 1977.

10 D Smith in *The Education of Travellers Children* ed H Steyne and D Derrick, Centre for Information and Advice on Educational Disadvantage, 1977.

11 ILEA Teachers for Travellers, *Travellers and Education in Inner London*, 1989 p4.

12 GLC Briefing Document, *Background information for people working on unauthorised sites*.

13 Thomas Acton, *Gypsies*, p12.

14 Judith Okely, p5.

## Jon Cannon

Jon Cannon is a writer. He works in oral and community history and as a Company Member of Emergency Exit Arts writes lyrics and plots for performance – as well as performing occasionally himself. His own writing is rooted in his enthusiasm for travelling, place and history.

Travellers:
An Introduction

## InterChange

Based in Kentish Town, North London, InterChange is a locally based, national development agency. It provides a wide range of development services and facilities, including media resources, community architects, management training, youth arts and much more.

As a registered charity, the trust provides a wide range of advice and training services. They are designed to support community organisations of all kinds, from local community groups, co-operatives and small businesses to national charities, campaign groups and arts organisations.

## InterChange Books

InterChange books are aimed at helping groups and individuals to organise themselves more effectively and achieve their own objectives. Drawing on InterChange's wide experience of community work, InterChange books are practical and clearly written handbooks which make areas such as law, publishing and printing more accessible.

## Emergency Exit Arts

Emergency Exit Arts has gained a national reputation for unusual and innovative projects since it was formed in 1980. The multi-talented group, based in Southeast London, have invented amazing spectaculars, intimate touring grottos and fantastical street shows. They are likely to be found dreaming their schemes in public parks, derelict land, swimming pools and the odd ruined supermarket!

The company creates celebrations with fireworks, carnival processions, giant images and decorations. Skills as performers, musicians, artists, inventors, cooks and builders are shared through workshops and consultancies.

Emergency Exit Arts' highly visual style is aimed at a wide ranging audience and appeals to all ages. The work is powerful, entertaining and accessible. Each event is devised by the company and tailored specifically to an environment or community who are often encouraged to actively participate.

72

It's not they mind you Travelling. It's that everybody wants to own everything. You can't own the ground it sort of owns you don't it. The only bit of ground I'll ever hold is the one which puts me under.

Why is it all property? You don't own nothing really, you just borrows it.

*Bubbles Brazil*